NAVIGATING INDUSTRY 4.0

5 STEPS TO DIGITALISE MANUFACTURING AND INSPIRE INNOVATION

NAVIGATING INDUSTRY 4.0

5 STEPS TO DIGITALISE MANUFACTURING AND INSPIRE INNOVATION

By

ASHUTOSH PARASNIS

Worldwide Published by

Pendown Press

PENDOWN PRESS

An ISO 9001 & ISO 14001 Certified Co.,
Regd. Office: 2525/193, 1st Floor, Onkar Nagar-A, Tri Nagar, Delhi-110035
Ph.: 09350849407, 09312235086
E-mail: info@pendownpress.com
Branch Office: 1A/2A, 20, Hari Sadan, Ansari Road, Daryaganj, New Delhi-110002

Ph.: 011-45794768
Website: PendownPress.com

First Edition: 2020
Price: ₹259/-
ISBN: 978-93-90479-36-8

Layout and Cover Designed by Pendown Graphics Team
Printed and Bound in India by Thomson Press India Ltd.

CONTENTS

ABOUT THE AUTHOR

Business Strategist
Industry4.0/Digitalisation Catalyst
Innovation Coach

Founder-NewBox Consulting

Ashutosh Parasnis has worked in software & electronics manufacturing sectors in diverse functions such as R&D, manufacturing, supply-chain, software development, customer support & IT infrastructure. He was CEO at PTC & Qlogic India & has been associated with Stockholm School of Economics Executive Education & Symbiosis International University as Visiting Faculty. He is extremely passionate about innovation in Customer Experience, Business Management &

Technologies & has consulted enterprises, SMEs & start-ups in their transformation journey.

He is a speaker on Industry 4.0 and Innovation Management. He has authored industry articles and industry research report. His Strategy Development Framework, Readiness Assessments and Solution Design protocol are simple and effective tools that can be used to manage Industry 4.0 journey

He is an Electronics Engineer and MBA with specialisation in Marketing, Strategic Management and Business Process Re-engineering.

INTRODUCTION

Hello, I am Ashutosh Parasnis. I am a Business Strategist, Industry 4.0 Catalyst and Innovation Coach with over 30 years of experience.

My Tryst with Technology began with electronics, progressing to embedded electronics and software. For the past 15 years, my focus has been Business Strategy and Innovation management.

Having worked for companies that build hardware and software technologies for the manufacturing sectors, I got great insights about what works and what does not work.

Today, manufacturing techniques are undergoing major and rapid shifts globally, driven by Industry 4.0. It is triggering a significant structural change to the ways companies operate and their interactions with suppliers, customers and third parties.

In the last 5 years, I have worked with lots of manufacturing clients and other businesses and helped them in developing their Digitalised Business strategies and build capabilities for execution.

My interventions with clients have created results that include:

- **Revenue growth:** A renewed business strategy that improved revenues and customer acquisitions.
- **Cost of Quality:** A strategy shift from localised testing methods to Quality system using digital technology for improved compliance and audit process, quick search and retrieval of records, early alerts to reduce Cost of Quality, etc
- **Productivity, Cost Reduction:** Digital adoption in transactional process that improved productivity, employee motivation while reducing costs.
- **Capability Building for Industry 4.0:** Mindset, new thinking and new ideas amongst leadership and employees through capability workshops.
- **Innovation:** Scaling up of patentable ideas that contributed to monetisation as well as risk mitigation in business.

In this period, I have developed strategy frameworks, assessment methodologies, solution design tools as well as workshop content that develop meaningful roadmaps.

So, why am I writing this mini book?

I have met 3 kinds of manufacturers—those who are Industry 4.0 aware, those who are unaware and then there are those who are undecided or confused.

I therefore want to help manufacturers understand what Industry 4.0 is about, and how to approach it methodically.

So, they implement what is relevant to them and avoid wasting resources in non-value-add activities.

In turn, it can help them realistically visualise and design their own strategy and roadmap. The end result will be eliminating waste of time and money in unwanted activities.

When manufacturers develop this capability, they will truly be in-charge of the future of their business.

Hopefully, this mini book will activate your thought process and bring clarity that is meaningful for YOUR business.

So, without further delay, let us explore the 5 dimensions of Industry 4.0 that matter the most.

–Ashutosh Parasnis

BEFORE YOU START READING...

This book is written keeping in mind the manufacturing companies that are keen to initiate Industry 4.0 journey. However, others may find it useful as well.

As you step into the world of Industry 4.0, you will come across multiple terms that may be new to you. And covering the entire scope of this topic can be overwhelming. This mini book therefore addresses those aspects that are needed to start the journey. Given below are these aspects:

1. **Industry 4.0**, a term that originated in Germany, is also referred by multiple names. Some refer to it as **The Fourth Industrial Revolution**, though in reality there is a subtle distinction. You will also hear the term **Industrial Internet of Things** or **IIoT**. This refers to the networking of manufacturing devices. Industry 4.0 on the other hand aims at a connected value chain in manufacturing, thus making its scope larger than IIoT.

2. The other set of terms that are used frequently and at times interchangeably are digitisation, digitalisation and digital transformation.

Keep in mind the differences

Digitisation is when you convert a physical artefact into a digital one. Example: Collect product test data and store it in digital form.

Digitalisation is about improving a process with the help of stored data and additional technology. For example, the ability to digitally search and retrieve digital test records with a certain title, keyword, image or over a time period and analyse them.

Digital transformation is about changing the business model itself to leverage the advantages of digitalisation. For example, it develops processes that can automatically collect product performance data during production and on the field, for remote monitoring and management.

This mini book has 7 chapters.

Chapter 1 discusses as to what Industry 4.0 is really about and why should you take notice.

Chapter 2,3,4,5,6 discuss the 5 dimensions that must be considered in Industry4.0 implementation. Ample examples and case studies illustrate the practical aspects.

Capability Compass: A set of critical questions you can answer for self assessment of your readiness to begin Industry 4.0 journey.

Chapter 7 summarises what business leaders should focus on to start their Industry 4.0 journey.

Digital Manufacturing Enterprise (DME) use Industry 4.0–enabled technologies to drive their processes across the value chain. DMEs differ from traditional firms in three key ways: the audience they engage, the degree of connection they maintain, and their monetization of the products and services they provide.

–Deloitte-CII report, 2018

Chapter 1

INDUSTRY 4.0: NOT JUST A BUNCH OF TECHNOLOGIES

Have you ever read as to how leading Indian manufacturing companies like Mahindra, Bharat Forge, Bajaj Auto, Asian Paints, Reliance have been adopting Industry 4.0? What exactly is it and why there is increased buzz around Industry 4.0?

Manufacturing world today is facing two challenges simultaneously—the first is a fundamental transformation of manufacturing that is taking place due to digital technologies, connectivity, customer preferences and accessibility to global markets.

Another is environmental issues, such as geo-politics; new regulations are frequently creating uncertainties that put additional pressure on businesses. Such uncertainties create sudden materials shortages, steep drops in demand and worker unavailability.

This is changing the very nature of HOW manufacturers will create value, starting now.

This points to one singular truth—manufacturers not only need to focus on their present for survival, but also on the future to discover new options for resilience and growth.

What is Industry 4.0 and what is it trying to achieve?

If you are reading this book, then most likely you are aware of what Industry 4.0 is about. If not, there is enough material available that discusses the Industry 4.0 concept in detail. But, here is the gist.

Manufacturing has evolved over many years from mechanised production (1st Industrial Revolution) to manufacturing that is personalised, connected and intelligent (4th Industrial Revolution) called Industry 4.0. While this practice is far from being mature, the adoption is happening at a rapid pace.

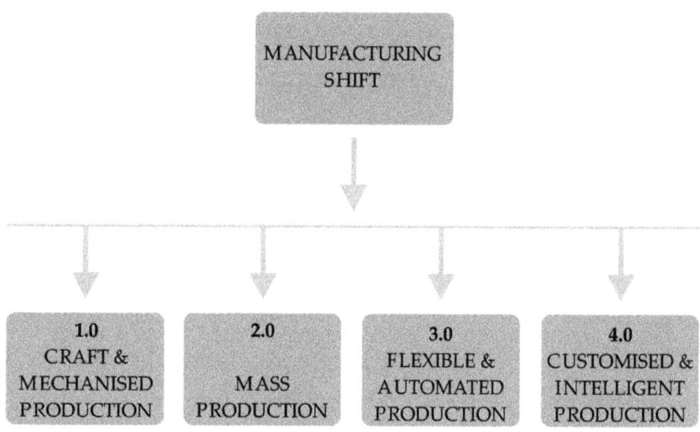

However, if I was to describe in single sentence, it would mean that Industry 4.0 will take the new technologies and connect the physical, digital and biological world together. This will be possible through connectivity, sensing, data collection and analysis to drive automation.

It offers opportunities to automate manufacturing, lower costs, reduce waste and offer quick response to changing scenarios of the market.

It also poses challenges of ability of people and systems to adapt to the changes.

Industry 4.0: The future mindset and management practice of manufacturing business:

Surveys are showing that Industry 4.0 adoption is growing globally across sectors. It is because Industry 4.0 was built on the idea of applying digital technologies to manufacturing. Many view Industry 4.0 as another digital technology approach. But, if you delve deeper, it is really about a new emerging management mindset and practice that is clearly going to be the backbone of tomorrow's manufacturing.

The technologies which are associated today with Industry 4.0 are critical enablers. They are the means, and not the end in themselves for achieving Industry 4.0 success. The technologies that exist today may suit one industry more than the others. Hence, we can see that Automotive sector leads the pack as compared to say, Textile industry.

But. what remains crucial is the mind shift that needs to happen to understand the trends, their impact on the future of your business and act accordingly.

TIPS

- Do not neglect Industry 4.0. It is the future of manufacturing.
- Industry 4.0 is about a new mindset and new management practice.
- Digital Technologies will play a crucial role to achieve Industry 4.0 success.
- If you are a part of such a manufacturing value chain, your business will most likely be impacted.

Strategy is about making choices, trade-offs; it is about deliberately choosing to be different.

– Michael Porter

Chapter 2

ARE YOU SHAPING YOUR STRATEGY?

Throughout my career, the one major learning that I have learnt is that STRATEGY matters. It provides a thought-out direction to your actions based on facts and researched estimates, rather than gut and impulse- to achieve a defined business outcome.

A related learning was that business value gets created when your initiatives are a part of the overall business strategy. Nano strategies within a function or a group, at most deliver some improvement, but do not make real impact.

Are you aware of the activities within your organisation that do not add any value and drain valuable time and money?

So, how should a strategy be developed? Here are the key steps that I recommend based on best practices in leading organisations.

1. Set the objectives that need to be achieved considering various trends. Apart from the financial objectives, companies should also set objectives that address Environmental and Social impacts to be achieved.
2. Conduct Assessments to identify Gaps.
3. Clearly state the inclusion of Industry 4.0 within your business.
4. Identify initiatives that meet the objectives, prioritise and secure funding.
5. Develop a meaningful and implementable roadmap.
6. Train your workforce so that it gets aligned with the roadmap.
7. Review frequently and correct as and when necessary.

The Need for an Integrated Strategy

A strategy is developed to achieve the desired business outcome. The four dominant outcomes are Revenue and Profit Growth, Healthy Cash flows, Enhanced Customer Experience and Compliances. Our approach to develop an integrated strategy for such outcomes is to strike the right balance between business needs, technology choice and innovation : the three faces of the "Value Creation Triangle".

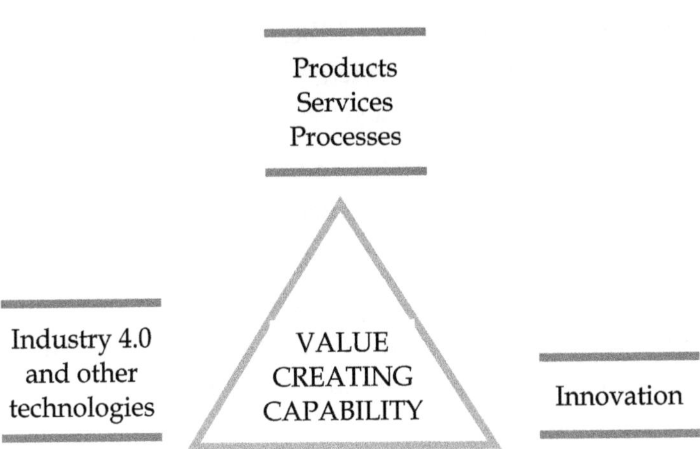

This approach ensures that a holistic view of the business is taken into consideration. Priorities are recognised, helping you in resource planning more effectively. It helps you to determine where money needs to be invested, where human resources are to be deployed, which new capabilities need to be developed so on and so forth. In the absence of an integrated view, desired results are unlikely to be achieved.

Did you notice that the list above includes Industry 4.0 and Innovation in steps 3 & 4?

My Client's Story

Let me illustrate this with an example of one of my client from the SME sector. The client was in business for a couple of decades, but was struggling with stagnant growth. Not being satisfied with status quo, he was passionate to get to the next level.

The Founder/CEO invited me for a strategic discussion. The conversation soon turned into serious project. After identifying the firm's objectives of the desired future state, we reviewed their then business model.

Having thoroughly analysed their offerings, customers and operations, newer insights emerged. A major insight was the absence of technology leverage.

Armed with these insights and years of experience in the industry, they developed a roadmap, including the bold step to adopt technology.

Initially, they automated business processes that boosted their employee productivity while improving candidate and client interaction. This resulted in revenue growth and customer stickiness.

Today, this integrated strategy approach, coupled with a refreshed mind set, is creating many opportunities for them in a digitally enabled business. It also helped in keeping their business active during pandemic lockdown.

TIPS

- Develop a Dynamic Integrated Strategy that aligns with market shifts in a timely manner.
- Make Industry 4.0 part of executive discussions.
- One-time, siloed and fragmented approach rarely creates long-lasting value.

Digital is the main reason just over half of the companies on the Fortune500 have disappeared since the year 2000

– Pierre Nanterme, Past CEO Accenture

Chapter 3

WHICH DIGITAL TECHNOLOGIES MATTER FOR YOU?

Today all of us are well versed, as users, with e-commerce and Internet Banking. Unlike in the past, these methods provide you the transparency and control at any time of the day. This sea-change has been made possible by digital and networking technologies. This is IT (Information Technology) as we know it.

Factories too have their world of digital and networking technologies in the form of PLC, SCADA, Industrial Ethernet, etc. This is referred as OT (Operational Technology). Industry 4.0 integrates IT with OT.

The following wheel depicts the digital technologies, that are most popular today. Note that sensors, robotics and 3D-printing would be a part of OT, while Cloud, Analytics and network security will get classified as IT in Non- Industry4.0 environment.

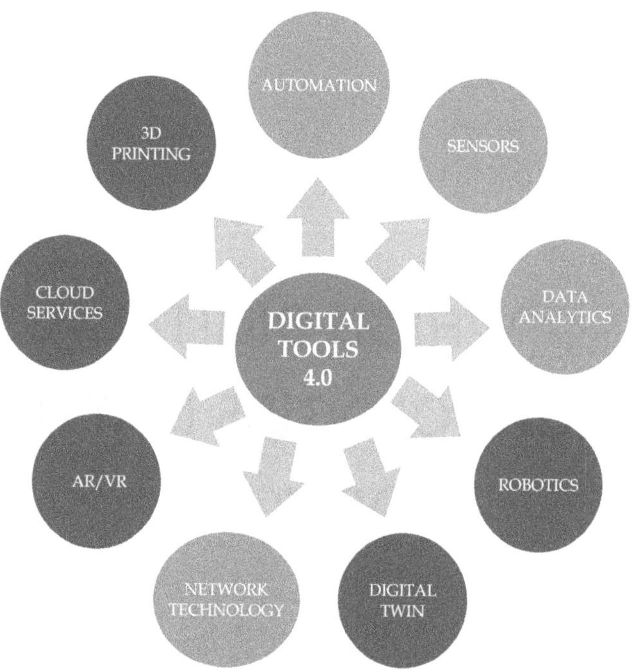

However, to begin with, it is recommended to get conversant with four digital technologies: **Automation, Sensors, Data Analytics and Networking technologies.**

Robotics is already in use in manufacturing companies, especially medium and large ones.

Another manufacturing technology that is growing rapidly is **Additive manufacturing** or **3D printing**. It has not yet become a part of manufacturing process, but is used in rapid prototyping and fulfilling after sales requirements.

Not all companies may be equipped with these capabilities, so the first task would be to get acclimatised with them at the earliest.

With the help of digital methods, here are some quick use cases that are known to reduce costs by 25%–40% and as a result, improve cash-flow.

Example: Sensor-based real time monitoring of manufacturing process replaces the manual readings and observations that are taken at longer intervals (Automation and smart sensors).

Smart sensors and cameras keep a watch on the progress of manufacturing, quality of parts, assemblies as they flow through or variations that take place in manual operations. Such data that may not be monitored by PLCs, can be analysed in real time and used to manage quality and productivity. Data gathered over time, is also analysed to discover trends in process flow and results (Data Analytics).

Example: With vibration sensors, motors can be monitored. Data analysis can not only give you early warning, but can also point out to the possible source of problem. The problem can be corrected early, thus avoiding an expensive break down.

During in-process monitoring of parts in production, such methods can similarly point out inconsistencies at an early stage, eliminating wastage and improving quality.

Visualisation, anywhere: One of our clients' integrated production data in one of the units. The data gathered was about which process was active, the health check of every machine, the status of air pressure-temperature-humidity needed for the process, etc. This was displayed on a central interactive display on the shop floor. Managers had access to same information on their mobiles (Networking technologies). Variations were highlighted visually in real-time helping the staff to respond ahead of any failures.

Analytics: Over time, with multiple sensors acquiring data, computers analyse it at the individual level and also for interdependency and correlation with data from other sensors. For example, our team designed a solution to demonstrate how a problem in quality of a finished part can be quickly correlated to a loose bearing in a motor of a drilling machine monitored by a vibration sensor.

Such data from multiple sources that gets collected and analysed on a single platform, forms the basis of an IoT platform in Industry 4.0.

As you can see, technologies can help in saving costs. The above examples are quite popular with companies that start their Industry 4.0 journey. This is because these use-cases are well understood. It does not need exceptionally large investments. Such quick wins build confidence and motivate businesses to explore additional deployment of digital tools.

As you get comfortable in the new environment, you start implementing projects that create new revenues, reduce cost of quality and compliance and deliver superior customer experience.

In the long run, you can create your own competitive advantage.

TIPS

- Digital technologies create new opportunities to save costs, generate revenue and improve cash flow.
- There are many digital technologies out there. All may not be relevant for every manufacturer.
- Get well versed with digital technology and its applications. Automation, Smart Sensors, Data Analytics and Networking technologies are a good starting point.
- You do not have to be an expert in Digital technology.
- Aim for small projects that can provide quick results at minimal costs, not complex projects.

Business Processes reinforce behaviours and mental models of managers in that industry. This is the reason why an intellectual understanding of the need and a desire for change are not enough. The firm needs the administrative capacity to execute that.

–C.K. Prahalad, M.S. Krishnan

Chapter 4

BUSINESS PROCESSES IN A DIGITAL WORLD

As manufacturers transition to world where customer demand personalisation, the nature and sources of competitive advantage will change. Examples of sources available to manufacturers include capital, material, technology, talent, infrastructure, etc. Historically, access to capital and raw material were sources of competitive advantage. In a globalised economy, everyone gained access to capital and raw material. The next competitive advantage was technology and talent. That too became ubiquitous.

Today, in a world where access to resources are available to manufacturers simultaneously, the question is: what is the unique source of competitive advantage?

Example: Let us compare the now famous example of Netflix and a TV channel that broadcasts movies. Both companies have access to same resources. Yet the popularity of Netflix outstrips the TV channel.

Example: Sony, Apple and Philips all made MP3 players. But the race was won by Apple by introducing i-tunes along with a superlative product design that drove clients crazy.

Both companies created a difference through a Business Process that delighted the customers and rattled the competition.

Using the same resources differently and innovatively, these companies deliver a personalised service across the world, primarily through Digital and Networking technologies. It not only disrupted their own business model; it has also disrupted the market.

So, what is a Business Process?

All activities in the company that convert strategy into action are called business processes. They include all department and functions. The success of your business depends on how these processes work in a collaborative and dynamic manner.

Example: Bajaj Auto has established a Center of Excellence in Data Analytics. This center is gathering and analysing data from the field on a continued basis. The analysis gives them insights about product and channel performance during sales and support cycles. The strategic intent is to deliver the best customer experience. This is very vital in their B2C market.

As one can see, with products becoming ubiquitous, businesses today are creating competitive advantage by re-imagining their business processes. In fact, the line between products and services is blurring rapidly where manufacturers provide "Product as a Service" and service companies provide "Service as a Product."

A significant part of this process has moved online with digitalisation.

My Client's Story

This is an example of how use of in-line power sensing devices revealed the energy consumption pattern in a large data center. The acquired data was able to point out the energy consumption at a granular level. Further analysis revealed that unused machines were also left on, wasting power consumption. This helped the company introduce an Energy Consumption Weekly Report to its mangers. It also identified unused equipment and its removal, thus releasing precious space to accommodate future expansion. This exercise saved lacs of rupees of the client.

Such transformation is being made possible in the Digital world. These approaches help you build relevant products and services, improve customer engagement and operational efficiency, thus putting you on the path of resilient growth.

TIPS

- Business Processes are the source of Competitive Advantage
- Business processes should be reviewed frequently to get aligned with market shifts. Digital technologies facilitate re-imagining of business processes.
- Always ask, can new value be created by doing things differently?

It's tough when markets change and your people within the company don't.

–Harvard Business Review

Chapter 5

IS YOUR TALENT READY?

The strategy for embracing Industry 4.0 clearly requires new skills and an ability to deal with change.

Industry 4.0 will drive a change in the nature of jobs. With technology taking over routine tasks earlier done manually by people, there is a need to tap the potential of higher order capabilities of people.

To manage transition to Industry 4.0, you will need to develop new capabilities across the organisation. The focus must be on the skills of individuals and their attitude towards learning.

Here is what World Economic Forum has to say about the requirement of new skills in Industry 4.0 era.

2022 SKILLS OUTLOOK

(Source World Economic Forum)

What will Grow	What will Decline
• Analytical thinking Critical thinking • Creativity and innovation • Technology design • Complex Problem solving • Leadership and social influence • Systems Analysis • Emotional intelligence	• Need for Manual Skills • Traditional Communication and cognitive skills • Routine management of financial material resources and personnel • Manual QC and safety tracking • Technology installation and maintenance • Coordination and time Management roles

This makes it amply clear that Capability Building is an important criterion to make the transition to Industry 4.0.

One option is to replace people with redundant skills with those having new skills. However, that is not desirable from a social perspective and not easy considering the labour regulations.

Even if that is implemented to some extent, it is not easy to find the new talent easily in the market.

It is therefore prudent that companies start planning to upskill their existing talent. If capability building is a part of the overall business strategy, it yields phenomenal results such as:

- The resistance to change from employees vanishes
- Company retains its experienced and loyal employees
- Job contraction reduces to organic attrition and retirement

- New recruitment narrows down to specialised skills such as data analysts, digital marketers.

My Client's Story

- In December 2019, a large manufacturing company invited us for Industry 4.0 capability building for its manufacturing unit. The challenge given by the management was not just to impart the subject matter training but also to help in exciting the employees about their new future and remove the fear of job loss due to automation.
- We had to adjust to this requirement in a short time and design workshops to train 450 employees that created the desired outcome. We quickly had to reconfigure our workshop content, activities and methodology.
- At the end of the day, not only the participants acquired the needed knowledge but started generating a lot of ideas about what can be achieved, during the workshop itself. Clearly, a positive impact for people and the business.

TIPS

- Industry 4.0 will need new skills.
- Include Capability building as a part of your strategy. Upskilling existing employees has many business benefits.

Continued Innovation is the best way to beat competition.

–Thomas Edison

Chapter 6

TIME TO DROP THE INNOVATION INERTIA

Let me start by making a bold statement!

If you start taking actions considering the pointers provided in earlier chapters, there is no better time than now to build the innovation culture.

A few years ago, when I tried to introduce the concept of innovation with a client there was a lot of enthusiasm during the meetings. A proposal was drawn up, but no one came forward to lead, when it came to execution. Not surprisingly, the company has shown no growth for the past 4 years, while the peer companies were growing at 6%–10%.

But today, the urgency to innovate is amply evident. Digitalisation, Competition and the new-age customer are forcing businesses to innovate. And those who do not, will stay afloat for some time but eventually be rejected by customers.

Innovation can happen anywhere in the business, not just products—innovations in supply chain, marketing, customer support, machine maintenance, employee training, safety and ultimately business models that are influencing business outcomes.

Example: Philips Lighting was originally creating products. They later on moved into providing solutions. Not only did they sell products, they also created a product and service bundle called Lifecycle solutions with its own pricing. Corporate customers had a choice to buy a complete package of lights, service, replacements for a subscription fee, etc. Later, Philips spun off this business. The new company now not only sells the earlier products and services but has also added "connected lighted systems" for variety of applications on an IoT platform. The new entity has shown positive results of profit growth and free cashflows, even in the midst of Covid-19 pandemic.

Your business will only benefit, if you create an environment of innovation within your company. Valuable insights and ideas come from those who are closest to the situation.

Be aware that balancing innovation (the future revenue) with operations (the present revenue) too needs a strategy and leadership. Management practices that are established for operations cannot be used to manage innovation.

In the new world, therefore leaders too need to develop themselves as much as other contributors.

My Client's Story

There are times when entrepreneurs create products first and then take them to the market. One such manufacturing start-up found out that their innovation did not yield desired results.

During review, it was discovered that while they had a wonderful product, it was expensive and hence accessible to a small target segment and hence not sustainable. When this observation became visible, the need for follow-up innovation in product design for a wider market was needed. This validated the point that innovation too needs a strategy to succeed.

That is why I have emphasised earlier the need for an Integrated Strategy that includes Business, Digital Technologies and Innovation. The earlier this becomes a part of the organisation culture, the better prepared businesses will be for the future.

TIPS

- Innovation Strategy is no longer a choice.
- Everyone across the organisation should be trained to innovate. Managing innovation and operations are two different things.

CAPABILITY COMPASS

QUESTIONS TO ASK

If the answers to ALL questions below is YES, you have clarity of your needs. You should activate your journey as soon as possible.

If some of your answers are NO, you have then identified the gaps that need to be bridged right away.

1. Are Digital practices important for the future of my business?
2. Am I well aware of the scope and applications of Industry 4.0?
3. Have I finalised the relevant Digital Technologies for my business?
4. Am I willing to change existing processes for future benefit?
5. Have I identified the projects for digital implementation?
6. Do these projects have a business plan?
7. Do I have access to the expertise needed for design and implementation?
8. Do I believe that business has to adapt more quickly and continuously in the future, than in the past?
9. Do I have an integrated strategy to digitalise my business?

Chapter 7

AGENDA FOR BUSINESS LEADERS

This brings us to the end of assessing the need for Industry 4.0. Hope you enjoyed reading this book.

So, what are the next steps?

Going forward, business leaders should:

- Be sensitive to the transformation of manufacturing that is underway. So they can assess its impact across their value chain–from supplier to the customer.
- Realise that Industry 4.0 needs a new mindset and management approach.
- Avoid implementing random projects deemed as Industry 4.0.
- Build an Industry 4.0 and Innovation strategy as a part of the overarching Business strategy. This will help in

prioritising projects that create business value.

- Review Business Processes to create future Competitive Advantage.
- Should initially focus on understanding technologies such as smart sensors, automation, data analytics and networking technologies.
- Start with small in-house projects that can deliver quick results. Do not aim for a big change.
- Plan and invest in up-skilling the organisation for knowledge and skills needed for Industry 4.0

You have couple of choices in front of you.

Begin your Industry 4.0 journey or defer it to a later date. If you decide to begin, you can start on your own.

OR

If you wish to discuss this further, kindly reach out to us at Industry4@newbox-consulting.com You can set up a complimentary call as well as get an idea of how we can help you.

You may have noted what we have achieved through the client stories. Our services span Capability Building, Readiness Assessments, Strategy and Solution Design.

If you agree to what you have read and are looking for assistance to shape your Industry 4.0 strategy, we would love to be your partner in that journey. Thank you for reading and wish you the best of luck.

www.ingramcontent.com/pod-product-compliance
Ingram Content Group UK Ltd.
Pitfield, Milton Keynes, MK11 3LW, UK
UKHW021654190726
13853UKWH00001B/261